Working Animals

Therapy Animals

by Julie Murray

Dash!

2

LEVELED READERS

An Imprint of Abdo Zoom • abdobooks.com

Dash!
LEVELED READERS

Level 1 – Beginning
Short and simple sentences with familiar words or patterns for children who are beginning to understand how letters and sounds go together.

Level 2 – Emerging
Longer words and sentences with more complex language patterns for readers who are practicing common words and letter sounds.

Level 3 – Transitional
More developed language and vocabulary for readers who are becoming more independent.

THIS BOOK CONTAINS
RECYCLED MATERIALS

abdobooks.com

Published by Abdo Zoom, a division of ABDO, PO Box 398166, Minneapolis, Minnesota 55439.
Copyright © 2020 by Abdo Consulting Group, Inc. International copyrights reserved in all countries.
No part of this book may be reproduced in any form without written permission from the publisher.
Dash!™ is a trademark and logo of Abdo Zoom.

Printed in the United States of America, North Mankato, Minnesota.
052019
092019

Photo Credits: Alamy, Getty Images, iStock, Shutterstock
Production Contributors: Kenny Abdo, Jennie Forsberg, Grace Hansen, John Hansen
Design Contributors: Dorothy Toth, Neil Klinepier

Library of Congress Control Number: 2018963315

Publisher's Cataloging in Publication Data

Names: Murray, Julie, author.
Title: Therapy animals / by Julie Murray.
Description: Minneapolis, Minnesota : Abdo Zoom, 2020 | Series: Working
    animals | Includes online resources and index.
Identifiers: ISBN 9781532127359 (lib. bdg.) | ISBN 9781532128332 (ebook) |
    ISBN 9781532128820 (Read-to-me ebook)
Subjects: LCSH: Working animals--Juvenile literature. | Animals--Therapeutic
    use--Juvenile literature. | AAT (Animal-assisted therapy)--Juvenile literature.
Classification: DDC 615.8--dc23

Table of Contents

Therapy Animals

Therapy animals do important work. They help people heal. They also bring them comfort.

Dogs are the most common therapy animals. Some other kinds of animals can do these jobs too!

These animals bring people joy. They are also calming for people who have **anxiety**.

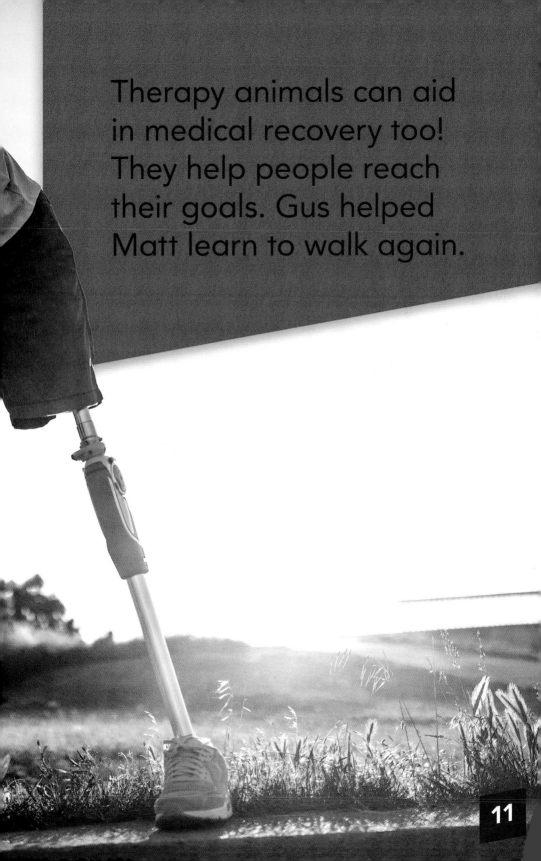

Therapy animals can aid in medical recovery too! They help people reach their goals. Gus helped Matt learn to walk again.

11

Where They Work

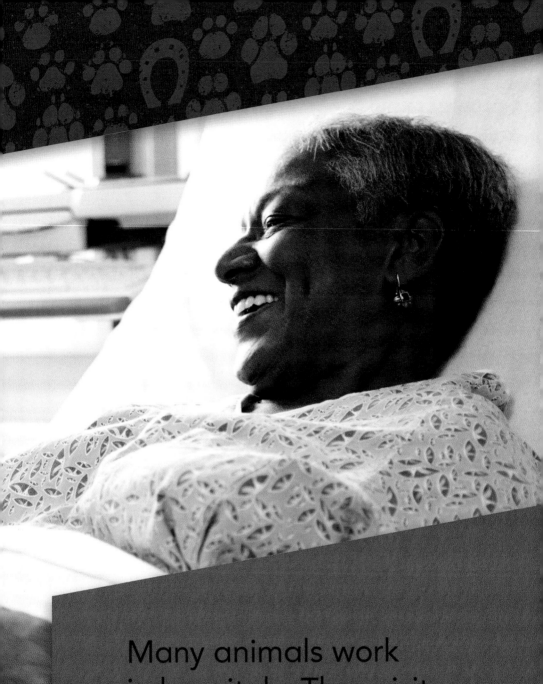

Many animals work
in hospitals. They visit
patients. Lucy sits with
Carrie on her bed.

Some work in nursing homes.
Felix sits on Jean's lap. Jean
enjoys petting him.

Dogs visit libraries. Sara enjoys reading out loud to Lou.

These animals also go to **disaster sites**. They bring comfort to emergency workers and others.

Sometimes people go where the animals live. Josh rides a **therapy horse** at a riding center.

- A dog named Smokey was one of the first therapy animals. He worked during WWII. He cheered up the soldiers by doing tricks.

- Therapy dogs were brought to the 9/11 site. They comforted police and fire fighters.

- Military veterans use therapy animals. The animal helps reduce a soldier's stress after returning from duty.

Glossary

anxiety – a medical disorder characterized by a state of excessive uneasiness, fear, and worry, typically with compulsive behavior and panic attacks.

disaster site – a place where a significant emergency has occurred such as a fire, flood, building collapse or other disruptive event.

therapy horse – a horse that helps patients develop needed skills like responsibility, confidence, and problem-solving through the patient's care of the horse.

Index

Online Resources

Booklinks
NONFICTION NETWORK
FREE! ONLINE NONFICTION RESOURCES

To learn more about therapy animals, please visit **abdobooklinks.com** or scan this QR code. These links are routinely monitored and updated to provide the most current information available.